D1528336

Super Cheap
Galápagos Islands
Travel Guide 2021

Our Mission

Like Simon Sinek said, "People don't buy what you do; they buy why you do it". We believe strongly that travel can and is best enjoyed on a budget.

If 2020 taught us anything it's this: Travel is a gift we must cherish and enjoy responsibly. The word responsible often evokes ideas of lavish spending. We have uncovered how to responsibly enjoy The Galápagos Islands on a tight budget.

Taking a trip to The Galápagos Islands is not just an outer journey, it's an inner one. Budget travel brings us closer to locals, culture and authenticity; which in turn makes our inner journeys more peaceful.

Travelling is painted as an expensive hobby; Travel guides, Travel bloggers and influencers often show you overpriced accommodation, restaurants and big-ticket attractions because they make money from our 'we're on vacation' mentality which leads to reckless spending. Our mission is to teach you how to enjoy more for less and get the best value from every dollar you spend in The Galápagos Islands.

This guide focuses on the cheap or free in The Galápagos Islands, but there is little value in travelling to The Galápagos Islands and not experiencing all it has to offer. Where possible we've included cheap workarounds or listed the experience in the loved but costly section - if it is worth your time and money.

We work to dispel myths, save you tons of money, teach you the local tips and tricks and help you find experiences in The Galápagos Islands that will flash before your eyes

when you come to take your last breath on this beautiful
earth.

Who this book is for and why anyone can enjoy budget travel

I've been travelling full-time for 20 years. I don't have a job and I'm not in any debt, which prompts friends and family to ask 'How can you afford to travel?'. My response? 'My passion is finding travel bargains'. This doesn't mean I do any less or sleep in dirty hostels. Someone who spends A LOT on travel hasn't planned or wants to spend their money. I believe you can live the bougie life on a budget; that's what I've been doing for the past 20 years.

Together with thrifty locals I met along the way I have funnelled my passion for travel bargains into 300 travel guides. In this guide, we have formulated a system to pass on to you, so you too can juice everything from visiting The Galapagos Islands while spending the least possible money.

There is a big difference between being cheap and frugal. I like to spend money on beautiful experiences, but 20 years of travel has taught me I could have a 20 cent experience that will stir my soul more than a $100 one. Of course, there are times when the reverse is true, my point is, spending money on travel is the best investment you can make but it doesn't have to be at levels set by hotels and attractions with massive ad spends and influencers who are paid small fortunes to get you to buy into something that you could have for a fraction of the cost.

I love travelling because it forces me to be present-minded. I like to have the cold hard budget busting facts to hand (which is why we've included so many one page charts, which you can use as a quick reference), but otherwise, I want to shape my own experience - and I'm sure you do too.

We have designed these travel guides to give you a unique planning tool to experience an unforgettable trip without spending the ascribed tourist budget.

When it comes to FUN budget travel, it's all about what you know. You can have all the feels without most of the bills. A few days spent planning can save you thousands. Luckily, Super Cheap Insider Guides have done the planning for you, so you can distill the information in minutes not days, leaving you to focus on what matters: immersing yourself in the sights, sounds and smells of The Galapagos Islands, meeting awesome new people and most importantly, feeling relaxed and happy. My sincere hope is that our tips will bring you great joy at a fraction of the price you expected.

So, grab a cup of tea, put your feet up and relax; you're about to enter the world of enjoying The Galapagos Islands on the cheap. Oh and don't forget a biscuit. You need energy to plan a trip of a lifetime on a budget.

Super Cheap Galápagos is <u>not</u> for travellers with the following needs:

1. You require a book with detailed offline travel maps. Super Cheap Insider Guides are best used with Google Maps - download before you travel to make the most of your time and money.
2. You would like thousands of accommodation, food and attraction recommendations; by definition, cheapest is most often singular. We only include maximum value recommendations. We purposively leave out over-priced attractions when there is no workaround.
3. You would like detailed write-ups about hotels/Airbnbs/Restaurants. We are bargain hunters first and foremost. We dedicate our time to finding the best deals, not writing flowery language about their interiors. Plus things change. If I had a pound for every time I read a Lonely Planet description only to find the place totally different, I would be a rich man. Always look at online reviews for the latest up to date information.

If you want to save A LOT of money while comfortably enjoying an unforgettable trip to the Galápagos islands, minus the marketing, hype, scams and tourist traps read on.

Redefining Super Cheap

The value you get out of Super Cheap The Galapagos Islands is not based on what you paid for it; its based on what you do with it. You can only do great things with it, if you believe saving money is worth your time. Charging things to your credit card and thinking 'oh I'll pay it off when I get back' is something you won't be tempted to do if you change your beliefs now. Think about what you associate with the word cheap, because you make your beliefs and your beliefs make you.

I grew up thinking you had to spend more than you could afford to have a good time travelling. Now I've visited 190 countries I know nothing is further from the truth. Before you embark upon reading our specific tips for The Galapagos Islands think about your associations with the word cheap.

Here are the dictionary definitions of cheap:

1. costing very little; relatively low in price; inexpensive:
a cheap dress.
2. costing little labor or trouble:
Words are cheap.
3. charging low prices:
a very cheap store.
4. **of little account; of small value; mean; shoddy:**
cheap conduct; cheap workmanship.
5. **embarrassed; sheepish:**
He felt cheap about his mistake.
6. **stingy; miserly:**
He's too cheap to buy his own brother a cup of coffee.

Three out of six definitions have extremely negative connotations. The 'super cheap' we're talking about in this book is not shoddy, embarrassed or stingy. Hey, you've already donated to charity just by buying this book - how is that stingy? We added the super to reinforce our message. Super's dictionary definition stands for 'a super quality'. Super Cheap stands for enjoying the best on the lowest budget. Question other peoples definitions of cheap so you're not blinded to possibilities, potential, and prosperity. Here are some new associations to consider forging:

Shoddy

Cheap stuff doesn't last is an adage marketing companies have drilled into consumers. However by asking vendors the right questions cheap doesn't mean something won't last, I had a $10 backpack last for 8 years and a $100 suitcase bust on the first journey. A   out of San Francisco University found that people who spent money on experiences rather than things were happier. Memories last forever, not things, even expensive things. And as we will show you during this guide you don't need to pay to create great memories.

Embarrassed

I have friends who routinely pay more to vendors because they think their money is putting food on this person's table. Paradoxically, Cuban doctors are driving taxi's because they earn more money; it's not always a good thing for the place you're visiting to pay more and can cause unwanted distortion in their culture - Airbnb pushing out renters is an obvious example. Think carefully about whether the extra money is helping people or incentivising greed.

Stingy

Cheap can be eco-friendly. Buying thrift clothes is cheap but you also help the Earth. Many travellers are often disillusioned by the reality of traveling experience since the places on our bucket-lists are overcrowded. Cheap can take you away from the crowds. You can find balance and harmony being cheap. Remember,"A journey is best measured in friends, rather than miles." – Tim Cahill. And making friends is free!

A recent survey by Credit Karma found 50% of Millennials and Gen Z get into debt travelling. **Please don't allow credit card debt to be an unwanted souvenir you take home.** As you will see from this book, there's so much you can enjoy in The Galapagos Islands for free and so many ways to save money! You just need to want to!

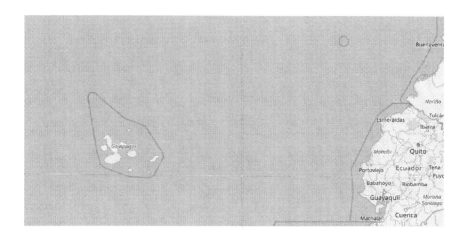

Discover The Galápagos Islands

In the 16the century the Galápagos islands were first mentioned in ship-logs of Pirates who started using the Galápagos as a hideout. Today it is a mecca for wildlife-viewing home to a spectacular diversity of plant and animal species, many found nowhere else.

The islands were never connected to mainland, so most species crossed 1000km of open ocean - only the fittest survived the trip.

Charles Darwin visited in 1835 and famously developed the 'Darwin theory of evolution' by observing Galápagos species.

You can visit the Galápagos Islands without an expensive tour. Fly into the Galápagos yourself and stay on Santa Cruz or San Cristobal - they are the busiest, most populated islands and hence cheaper. It is worth noting that the islands have only been inhabited 100 years, there is no real Latin American culture here, but there are over 400 species of fish surrounding the Galápagos Islands with more than 50 endemic species, including oysters, cuttlefish, snails, squids and octopuses making the Galápagos a seafood lover's paradise.

While the Galápagos Islands has the reputation of being among the most luxurious and expensive destinations in the world you can do a full DIY trip from $35 a day.

INSIDER CULTURAL INSIGHT

Goats introduced in the 1800s ate anything and everything on the islands, it became such a problem soldiers from New Zealand were drafted in to cull them up until 2006.

Some of The Galapagos Islands best bargains

Giant Tortoise for free

Use these coordinates 0°39'18.7"S, 90°24'34.3"W to see Giant Tortoise for free and in the wild. Be respectful of their habit and leave no trace.

Go snorkelling with sea lions

From La Loberia beach, on the outskirts of San Cristobal you can snorkel with sea lions for free!

Unique bargains I love in Galápagos Islands

The trick to keeping your trip cheap is to book a last minute cruise, in-person in Puerto Ayora on Santa Cruz to get out to the outer islands and off the tourist track. You do not need a $15,000 Luxury Cruse to see this beautiful Archipelago. While it is more expensive than the mainland, this destination is home to 25,000+ permanent residents who live on $10 a day.

NOTE: smoking is not allowed in the islands, but some travellers do light up on the sly.

 ## INSIDER INSIGHT

Bring your own supplies. Sunscreen and aftersun can run you $78 in Galápagos!

Planning your trip

The cheapest/best time to go

The first step in saving money on your Galápagos trip is timing. Go in April if possible. Prices are the lowest for tours. The Galápagos Islands are a year-round destination, so don't worry too much about timing. The hottest and wettest periods are March and April hence the lower prices.

Where to stay?

Santa Cruz Island is the most developed island in all Galápagos. Puerto Ayora is where most cruises and day tours depart. San Cristobal was the cheapest island I stayed on and the second most visited island in the Galápagos.

The cheapest place to stay

Stay in hostels or airbnbs they are similarly priced.

- If you're travelling solo hostels are your best option, both for meeting people and saving pennies. Galapagos Best Home Stay and Galapagos Best Hostel offer dorms from $12 a night.
- If you're travelling as a group or couple Airbnbs are the best bang for your buck. We stayed at this guest suite - https://www.airbnb.com/rooms/28497137?s=51 $18 a night.

Hack your Galápagos Accommodation

Your two biggest expenses when travelling to Galápagos are accommodation and food. This section is intended to help you cut these costs dramatically before and while you are in Galápagos.

Hostels are the cheapest accommodation in Galápagos but there are some creative workarounds to upgrade your stay on the cheap.

Use Time

There are two ways to use time. One is to book in advance. Three months will net you the best deal, especially if your visit coincides with an event. The other is to book on the day of your stay. This is a risky move, but if executed well, you can lay your head in a five-star hotel for a 2-star fee.

Before I travelled to Galápagos, I checked for big events using a simple google search 'What's on in Galápagos', there were no big events drawing travellers so I risked showing up with no accommodation booked (If there are big events on demand exceeds supply and you should avoid using this strategy) I started checking for discount rooms at 11 am using a private browser on booking.com.

Before I go into demand-based pricing, take a moment to think about your risk tolerance. By risk, I am not talking about personal safety. No amount of financial savings is worth risking that. What I am talking about is being inconvenienced. Do you deal well with last-minute changes? Can you roll with the punches or do you dislike it if something changes? Everyone is different and knowing yourself is the best way to plan a great trip. If you are someone that likes to have everything pre-planned using demand-based pricing to get cheap accommodation will not work for you. Skip this section and go to blind-booking.

Demand-based pricing

Be they an Airbnb host or hotel manager; no one wants empty rooms. Most will do anything to make some revenue because they still have the same costs to cover whether the room is occupied or not. That's why you will find many hotels drastically slashing room rates for same-day bookings.

How to book five-star hotels for a two-star price

You will not be able to find these discounts when the demand exceeds the supply. So if you're visiting during the peak season, or during an event which has drawn many travellers don't try this.

On the day of your stay, visit booking.com (which offers better discounts than Kayak and agoda.com). Hotel Tonight individually checks for any last-minute bookings, but they take a big chunk of the action, so the better deals come from booking.com. The best results come from booking between 2 pm and 4 pm when the risk of losing any revenue with no occupancy is most pronounced, so algorithms supporting hotels slash prices. This is when you can find rates that are not within the "lowest publicly visible" rate. To avoid losing customers to other websites, or cheapening the image of their hotel most will only offer the super cheap rates during a two hour window from 2 pm to 4 pm. Two guests will pay 10x difference in price but it's absolutely vital to the hotel that neither knows it.

Takeaway: To get the lowest price book on the day of stay between 2 pm and 4 pm and extend your search radius to include further afield hotels with good transport connections.

How to trick travel Algorithms to get the lowest hotel price

Do not believe anyone who says changing your IP address to get cheaper hotels or flights does NOT work. If you don't believe us, download a Tor Network and search for flights and hotels to one destination using your current IP and then the tor network (a tor browser hides your IP address from algorithms. It is commonly used by hackers). You will receive different prices.

The price you see is a decision made by an algorithm that adjusts prices using data points such as past bookings, remaining capacity, average demand and the probability of selling the room or flight later at a higher price. If booking.-com knows you've searched for the area before it will keep the prices high. To circumvent this, you can either use a different IP address from a cafe or airport or data from an international sim. I use a sim from Three, which provides free data in many countries around the world. When you search from a new IP address, most of the time, and par-ticularly near booking you will get a lower price. Sometimes if your sim comes from a 'rich' country, say the UK or USA, you will see higher rates as the algorithm has learnt people from these countries pay more. The solution is to book from a local wifi connection - but a different one from the one you originally searched from.

How to get last-minute discounts on owner rented properties

In addition to Airbnb, you can also find owner rented rooms and apartments on www.vrbo.com or HomeAway or a host of others. Nearly all owners renting accommodation will happily give renters a "last-minute" discount to avoid the space sitting empty, not earning a dime.

Go to Airbnb or another platform and put in today's date. Once you've found something you like start the negotiating by asking for a 25% reduction. A sample message to an Airbnb host might read:

Dear HOST NAME,

I love your apartment. It looks perfect for me. Unfortunately, I'm on a very tight budget. I hope you won't be offended, but I wanted to ask if you would be amenable to offering me a 25% discount for tonight, tomorrow and the following day? I see that you aren't booked. I can assure you, I will leave your place exactly the way I found it. I will put bed linen in the washer and ensure everything is clean for the next guest. I would be delighted to bring you a bottle of wine to thank you for any discount that you could offer.

If this sounds okay, please send me a custom offer, and I will book straight away.

YOUR NAME.

In my experience, a polite, genuine message like this, that proposes reciprocity will be successful 80% of the time. Don't ask for more than 25% off, this person still has to pay the bills and will probably say no as your stay will cost them more in bills than they make. Plus starting higher, can offend the owner and do you want to stay somewhere, where you have offended the host?

In Practice

To use either of these methods, you must travel light. Less stuff means greater mobility, everything is faster and you don't have to check-in or store luggage. If you have a lot of luggage, you're going to have fewer of these opportunities to save on accommodation. Plus travelling light benefits the planet - you're buying, consuming, and transporting less stuff.

Blind-booking

If your risk tolerance does not allow for last-minute booking, you can use blind-booking. Many hotels not wanting to cheapen their brand with known low-prices, choose to operate a blind booking policy. This is where you book without knowing the name of the hotel you're going to stay in until you've made the payment. This is also sometimes used as a marketing strategy where the hotel is seeking to recover from past issues. I've stayed in plenty of blind book hotels. As long as you choose 4 or 5 star hotels, you will find them to be clean, comfortable and safe. priceline.com, Hot Rate® Hotels and Top Secret Hotels (operated by lastminute.com) offer the best deals.

Hotels.com Loyalty Program

This is currently the best hotel loyalty program with hotels in Galápagos. The basic premise is you collect 10 nights and get 1 free. hotels.com price match, so if booking.com has a cheaper price you can get hotel.com, to match. If you intend to travel more than ten nights in a year, its a great choice to get the 11th free.

Don't let time use you.

Rigidity will cost you money. You pay the price you're willing to pay, not the amount it requires a hotel to deliver. Therefore if you're in town for a big event, saving money on accommodation is nearly impossible so in such cases book three months ahead.

The best price performance location in Galápagos

Galapagos Verde Azul in Puerto Ayora is a luxurious 4-hotel with consistent last minute rooms from $40 a night.

Use our FREE accommodation finder service

Feeling overwhelmed by all the accommodation options? Save yourself stress, hassle and time by using our FREE accommodation finder service.

We pride ourselves on actively helping our readers find the best price-performance accommodation. We normally charge $50 for this service, but for our paid readers it is FREE when you leave an honest review of this book. (Just a few short words like 'Excellent budget tips and insider insights' is all it takes).

So, how do you use the service?

Simply send our Services Manager, Amy Abraham the following information:

1. A screenshot proof of purchase. (Go to your Amazon account, and click orders and make a screenshot of your purchase.)
2. Send a screenshot of your review of the guide on Amazon.
3. And answers to the following questions:

- What's your Budget? (e.g. lowest possible)
- How many are travelling and what are their ages?
- What Approximate location do you desire? (e.g. as close to the centre as possible/ near public transport)
- Do you have a strong dislike of either hostels or Airbnbs?
- If anyone in your group has mobility restrictions/ requires a lift/ no stairs etc?
- Add any details you think are pertinent to your needs.

About Amy and her team

Amy has travelled to over 170 countries personally and has recruited a team of bargain hunters to provide our accommodation finder service.

Send your details via E-mail to Amy Abraham at Amy@supercheapinsiderguides.com

What you'll receive

Amy and her team will work their magic. Within 24 hours you will be sent a list of the top three accommodations for your specific needs prioritised by which one we recommend.

We offer the same service for finding you the cheapest most direct flight. See our cheapest route to The Galapagos Islands for details.

If you would like to follow us on Facebook you can find us here: https://www.facebook.com/SuperCheapInsiderGuides/ . We also accept accommodation search requests via Facebook messenger, just make sure you send the necessary information listed above.

(Please note: If you received this book for free as part of a promotion, we cannot extend this service to you.)

How to be a green tourist in The Galapagos Islands

The Galapagos Islands are an extremely fragile environment, easily affected by changes, so it's important as responsible tourists that we help not hinder The Galapagos Islands.

There is a bizarre misconception that you have to spend money to travel in an eco-friendly way. This like, all marketing myths was concocted and hyped by companies seeking to make money off of you. In my experience, anything with eco in front of their names e.g Eco-tours will be triple the cost of the regular tour. Don't get me wrong sometimes its best to take these tours if you're visiting endangered areas, but normally such places have extensive legislation that everyone, including the eco and non-eco tour companies, are complying with. The vast majority of ways you can travel eco-friendly are free and even save you money.

- Properly clean your clothes and shoes before you come to The Galapagos Islands. New bacterias can damage the fragile eco-system.
- Avoid Bottled Water - get a good water bottle and refill. The water in The Galapagos Islands is NOT safe to drink. Stay somewhere with a kettle or stove. You can then boil water, cool and refill safely. Single-use plastic is a big problem for The Galapagos Islands.
- Thrift shop but check the labels and don't buy polyester clothes - overtime plastic is released into the ocean when we wash polyester.
- Don't put it in a plastic bag, bring a cotton tote with you when you venture out.

- Pack Light - this is one of the best ways to save money. If you find a 5-star hotel for tonight for $10, and you're at an Airbnb or hostel, you can easily pack and upgrade hassle-free. A light pack equals freedom and it means less to wash.
- Travel around The Galapagos Islands on Bikes or e-Scooters or use Public Transportation.
- Walk, this is the best way to get to know The Galapagos Islands. You never know what's around the corner.
- Travel Overland - this isn't always viable especially if you only have limited time off work, but where possible avoid flying and if you have to compensate by off-setting or keeping the rest of your trip carbon-neutral by doing all of the above.

Saving money on Galápagos Food

Breakfast

If you stay somewhere with a free breakfast, eat smart. Don't eat sugary cereals or white flour rich pastries if you don't want to be hungry an hour later. Before leaving your hotel or checking out, find some fresh fruit, water, and granola in the fitness centre or coffee in the lobby or business centre. If your hotel doesn't have free breakfast, don't take it. You can always eat cheaper outside. Galápagos has the best cheap breakfast we found.

Opt for plata di dia
Most restaurants offer a plate of the day special for $3 - $5. More in the must-try foods section.

SNAPSHOT: How to enjoy a $2,000 trip to Galápagos Islands for $400

(full breakdown at the end of the guide)

Get there	fly LAN airlines $250 return from Quito or Guayaquil.
Stay	Guest suite - https://www.airbnb.com/rooms/28497137?s=51 $18
	Hostels from $12 a night or use our accommodation finder service.
Eat	Average meal cost: $3 – $6
Move	Buy a last minute five day cruise to the outer (and most interesting islands) from Puerto Ayora $180 for 3 days.
See	Entrance fees at the airport $100
Total	US$400* ($400 in total with flight there)

How to use this book

Google and Tripadvisor are your on-the-go guides while travelling, a travel guide adds the most value during the planning phase, and if you're without wifi. Always download the google map for your destination - having an offline map will make using this guide much more comfortable. For ease of use, we've set the book out the way you travel starting with arriving, how to get around, then on to the money-saving tips. The tips we ordered according to when you need to know the tip to save money, so free tours and combination tickets feature first. We prioritised the rest of the tips by how much money you can save and then by how likely it was that you would be able to find the tip with a google search. Meaning those we think you could find alone are nearer the bottom. I hope you find this layout useful. If you have any ideas about making Super Cheap Insider Guides easy to use, please email me philgattang@gmail.com .Now let's get started with juicing the most pleasure from your trip to The Galápagos Islands with the least possible money.

OUR SUPER CHEAP TIPS…

Poor mans Galápagos - Isla de la Plata

A trip to The Galápagos Islands will cost at a minimum $400. It's the most expensive part of a trip around South America, and in my experience is worth every penny. However, if this is really pushing your budget there is a 'Poor Man's Galápagos' - Isla de la Plata. With wildlife to match the Galápagos, but without the crowds and high prices. You can do a tour there which includes Walking on the island, seeing turtles and blue footed boobies and dolphins and seals on the way there and afterwards they normally take you snorkelling near a reef where theres turtles, but you also get to see a lot of amazing colourful-fish and the tour costs about $40. Most tours start in Puerto Lopez at 9am. Adventuras la Plata is a better known tour company charging $30 - $40 for a full day trip.

Get there via plane...

There are airports on three islands. Most people fly into Baltra Island.

Check LAN Airlines and TAME as they often have cheap flights, going for as low as $250 round-trip - start following LAN Airlines newsletter for deals.

BE AWARE: There's a park entrance fee of $100 charged at the airport in Galápagos. $100 MUST be paid in cash the moment you pass passport control.

Foreign tourists, non-residents of Ecuador over 12 years	US $100
Foreign tourists, non-residents of Ecuador under 12 years	US $50
Foreign tourists non-residents of Ecuador over 12 years, nationals of one of the countries belonging to the Andean Community of Nations or Mercosur	US $50
Foreign tourists non-residents of Ecuador under 12 years, nationals of one of the countries belonging to the Andean Community of Nations or Mercosur	US $25
Tourists and foreign nationals residing in Ecuador, over 12 years	US $6
Tourists and foreign nationals residing in Ecuador, under 12 years	US $3
Tourists, students not living in Ecuador who are enrolled in national educational institutions	US $25

If you need help finding a cheap flight, simply review this book and email me to find you the cheapest most direct flight.

- There's an additional $20 transit control fee charged before checking in for your flight in Guayaquil or Quito.
- It's not possible to buy a one-way ticket without proof of transportation from the islands. While this is true, I spoke with travelers who managed to fly into Galápagos with only a one-way ticket (but maybe they were lucky) so buy a return to avoid problems.

Suggested itinerary

If you're visiting the Galápagos Islands to be enthralled by all her unique wildlife, this itinerary ensures the best use of your time.

Day 1: Arrived in Santa Cruz in the afternoon, have a taxi take you to El Chato Reserve for lava tubes and tortoises and continued onto the hotel (Semilla Verde in the highlands, complete with tortoises just outside of your room).

Day 2: Santa Cruz - Charles Darwin Breeding Center and snorkeling at Las Grietas.

Day 3: Spent the day at Tortuga Bay. Walked in and took the boat back to town (~$8.50-$10 per person).

Day 4: Day trip to Pinzon (the place to see and snorkel with sea lions, sea turtles, sting rays and white tipped sharks)

Day 5: Traveled to Isabela Island, checked in at the Isabela Beach House (with a room that steps out onto the beach, and iguanas everywhere), walked to the tortoise breeding centre and saw flamingos.

Day 6: Wake up early for Los Tuneles Tour (blue footed boobies, sea turtles, caves full of white tipped sharks, seahorses, manta rays and sting rays, and one penguin). In the afternoon, snorkelled at Concha Perla in town. The beach has tons of sea lions and if you're lucky you'll find a shark or manta day when snorkelling.

Day 7: Do a kayaking/snorkel tour to Las Tintoreras in the morning. There were a few golden rays and penguins on the way back and some sea lions and iguanas, but overall didn't think this tour was anymore valuable than the other snorkeling excursions.
In the afternoon, we biked to the Wall of Tears, and on the way, saw an elephant seal who was lost from Antarctica. I highly recommend this bike ride (or walk) when visiting Isabela. Don't skip Isabela when visiting the Galapagos.

Day 8: Returned to Santa Cruz (Hotel - Cucuve Suites) and had a relaxing day, with some time spent observing at the fish market and some time spent on the Station Beach.

Day 9: Day trip to North Seymour Island. This was very cool for the frigate birds and land iguanas (and more blue footed boobies). We saw one flamingo when we stopped at Bachas Beach. However, this excursion is expensive and the snorkelling was cool for fish and not much else, so unless your heart is set on frigate birds and land iguanas, skip this to save money.

Day 10: Spent some time at Playa de Los Alemanes in the morning and then fly back to Quito. Make sure you have your exit paper they gave you when you arrived at the airport.

Arriving

Getting from the Airport.

When you land on Baltra Island, take the public bus signed 'Muelle' to the dock (a free 10- minute ride). Then take the ($1) ferry to Santa Cruz island. From where the ferry drops you take a bus ($2) to Puerto Ayora.

Getting Around

Although it can get a bit hilly, walking distances are reasonable for a fit traveller. You can take buses around the islands for $2 a ride.

Ferries between the islands are the cheapest way to island

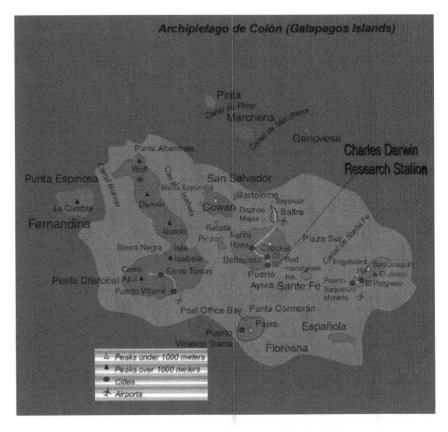

hop. Ferry tickets to Isabella and San Cristobal islands cost $30 each way. When going to Isabella, the ticket cost doesn't include the $1 per person water taxi to get to the boat and to get to the pier. So you will have to pay $1 to get to your boat and $1 to get off. When arriving on Isabella, they'll also charge you $10 tourist fee that goes to the island. When going to San Cristobal you won't have to pay for water taxis or an extra $10 fee.

Note: When leaving an island to visit another island your bags will be searched to ensue you're not bringing any thing dangerous to the ecology of the islands. Don't bring anything with seeds.

💡 INSIDER MONEY SAVING TIP

Try Geocaching

This is where you hunt for hide-and-seek containers. You need a mobile device to follow the GPS clues in Galápagos. A typical cache is a small, waterproof container with a logbook where you can leave a message or see various trinkets left by other cache hunters. Build your own treasure hunt by discovering geocaches in Galápagos. www.-geocaching.com

Look here for a last minute cruise

Cruises are the best way to reach the most beautiful and untouched islands in Galápagos - Fernandina and Genovesa.

The best place to find a cheap one is in Puerto Ayora. When you arrive search there for a cruise - you can get up to 50% off when booking last minute and in person. Imagine Ecuador offered the best last minute deals in late 2019.

A 5 day cruise is currently around US$800 meaning with a 50% discount you can save $400. You can also do numerous day trips from a base island (costing $50-$100; be prepared to haggle for those).

How to haggle. You can save a lot by haggling for your tour. Start low and work your way to the middle. When you walk away, the person you're haggling with, will call you back, and this is when you will get the lowest price. The best prices can be had at

4pm the day before the tour. Put simply, they want to fill the spaces.

NOTE: this is only a good idea if you are travelling alone or as a pair. Groups should be prepared to separate.

BEWARE: When you book your cruise in Puerto Ayora do it at a physical place. There are people who will claim to be cruise providers - who are not.

INSIDER CULTURAL INSIGHT

Giant tortoise's feel into steep decline due to how tasty they were. They have the ability to live without food or water for months so were often take on long voyages as meat to feed soldiers. Fortunately tortoises are now a protected species.

Eat at Los Kioskos Market

The most delicious and economical place to eat on Santa Cruz and they serve Lobster! If you plan to eat at restaurants go for the lunch menu of the day - menu del dia - to save money.

Address: Calle 23 De Octubre y Chimborazo, Puerto Ayora

Eat at bakeries

Bakeries around the islands make for a cheap breakfast or snack. Sabor Cuencano Bakery and Coffee Shop was my favourite.

Pro tip: Doing laundry is super cheap on all the islands. I paid less than a dollar for 5 kilos.

Free or cheap: Puerto Ayora

1. Charles Darwin Station

Hike there from Puerto Ayora. There is a turtle breeding area and interesting conservation information about the unique biosphere of Galápagos. And it's FREE!

2. Go to Tortuga Bay

Look out for marine turtles, pelicans, marine iguanas, and Blue Heron.

3. Go snorkelling on German beach

If you are lucky you might spot small sharks. You can find cheap snorkelling gear around the town. I paid $5.

4. Visit Lava Tunnels

The biggest are located on private property off farms near Bellavista or Santa Rosa and cost $5 to visit.

5. Garrapatero Beach

A 20-minute bus from Puerto Ayora, then a 20-minute trail leads to this unique beach consisting of black lava, white sand, and a turquoise sea. Ask at your hostel about where you can take the bus.

6. Explore the Santa Cruz Fish Market

Markets are a fun and eye-opening plunge into local culture and, unless you succumb to the persistent vendors, it will cost you nothing.

Visit tortoise farms

There are two tortoise farms on Santa Cruz that you can do yourself and you don't have to pay for an expensive tour with a big group. You can either hire a taxi and driver for $35 to take you there and wait for you. Or you can take a local bus $0.50/$1 to drop you off by the side road and then walk for 1hr to the farm. It's a safe walk, down a gravel road where you will see cows and horses and we even saw a tortoise outside of the farm barrier. If you do this, bring water and rain gear because you're in the highlands and it rains often. The tortoise farm entry fee is $7 and they can give you rubber boots if needed.

Wildlife to spot

- Giant Tortoise
- Iguanas
- Flamingos
- Blue footed boobies (they're birds)
- Great frigate birds - they have giant red necks - see below.
- Sea Lions

Worth the fee: Dive at Gordon Rocks

Gordon Rocks is the highlight of any Galápagos diving experience. The locals call it the washing machine. Here you can see
many hammerhead sharks and whale sharks. It is at the top of a
submerged cone at the northeastern end of Santa Cruz Island. A
day day starts at $120.

Free things to in San Cristóbal

The public ferries cost between $25US per passenger. It's best to check with a couple of ticket sellers in Puerto Ayora (you will see signs for ferry tickets everywhere) before buying your tickets.

San Cristóbal is the second most visited island in the Galápagos. The island was founded in 1880. It grew in importance when Manuel Cobos opened a sugar factory in 1891. He 'hired' jailed mainlanders to work for him. Unfortunately for him, they railled against his enforced slavery and killed him in1904. You can visit the ruins of the factory and see where he is buried in the village of El Progresso.

Nearby is Lake El Junco Lagoon. It's one of the few permanent freshwater bodies in the Galápagos. I went there by public bus which runs on Sundays.

San Cristóbal is home to the nicest beaches in the Galápagos:

- **Cerro Brujo** is a white sand beach home to a colony of sea lions and blue- footed boobies.
- **Ochoa Beach** is where you can see sea lions.
- **Las Tijeretas bay** is a rock bay with excellent snorkeling.

Interpretation Center is a free museum explaining the biology, geology and human history of the islands. Playa Mann is a small beach popular in front of the musuem.

Escape the crowds

The Galapagos Islands has many hidden gems that aren't com-mercialized or too crowded most of the time. Here are the best:

1. La Lobería - a 10 minute drive from Puerto Baquerizo Moreno on San Cristobal you will find thousand os sea lions and their pups dozing on rocks.
2. Seymour is home to the amazing Blue Footed Boobies.
3. Kicker Rock is a great diving and snorkelling spot. The waters are choppy but you'll find rays and turtles.
4. Puerto Villamil is Isabela's main settlement provides an oppor-tunity to step back to a simpler time. Here you won't find an ATM but the side streets are made from lava rock. From here you can visit Las Tintoreras - a small collection of islets. They are home to sea turtles, penguin and hammerhead sharks

Is the tap water drinkable?

No. Drink bottled or filtered water only.

Haggle-o-meter

How much can you save haggling here?

You can save 50% in low season haggling for tours.

Enjoy your first Day for under $20

After landing on Santa Cruz, pay your fees and then Start with a croissant and coffee from the Galápagos Deli in Puerto Ayora (**Address:** Thomas de Berlanga, Puerto Ayora, Ecuador). Put your stuff down at your hostel and Then go to Av Charles Darwin to talk to travel agents about getting a last minute cruise. After that grab lunch at **Los Kioskos market**. Then go and see the Charles Darwin station. Head home for a rest. Eat some delicious dinner from Lo and Lo - We always had Bolones con Salsa for $6 and a pitcher of fresh juice. Watch the sunset at Tortuga Bay and go to bongo bar for a drink to round off your first day.

Websites to save you Money

1. **TalkTalkbnb.com** - Here you stay for free when you teach the host your native language
2. Rome2Rio.com - the go to site for good travel prices on train, bus, planes etc. Especially good for paths less travelled.
3. couchsurfing.com - stay for free with a local - always check reviews.
4. trustedhousesitter.com - always check reviews
5. booking.com - now sends you vouchers for discounts in the city when you book through them
6. airbnb.com for both accommodation and experiences.
7. hostelbookers.com - book hostels
8. www.latam.com/ - cheap flights.

Need to Know

Currency: US Dollar

Language: Spanish.

Money: Available ATMs but few in smaller islands. Beware American Express might not work here.

Visas: http://www.doyouneedvisa.com/

Mobile Data:

Time: GMT - 6

Important Numbers

112 Ambulance

112 Police

Watch to understand the History

Galápagos Islands's history is fascinating. There are tons of documentaries. This is a great watch - https://www.y-outube.com/watch?v=IoCFLfb66f8

Cheapest route to Galápagos from America

At the time of writing Avianca are flying roundtrip from Miami for $500 or one-way $320. I specialise in finding cheap flights, so if you need help finding a cheap flight simply review this book and send me an email. philgtang@gmail.com (Please send me a screenshot of your review - with your flight hacking request). I aim to reply to you within 12 hours. If it's an urgent request mark the email URGENT in the subject line and I will endeavour to reply ASAP.

From	To	Depart	Return
United States (Any)	Galapagos Is (GPS)	Cheapest mo...	(One Way)

Direct flights only (none)

Estimated lowest prices only. Found in the last 15 days.

Select departure city

Miami
1+ stops   from **$320** >

Fort Lauderdale
1+ stops   from **$323** >

Tampa
1+ stops   from **$382** >

Boston
1+ stops   from **$383** >

Cheapest route to Galápagos from Europe

At the time of writing Avianca are flying to Ecuador for around $500 return from Spain. You will need to take a flight from there to the islands, approx $200 return. I specialise in finding cheap flights, so if you need help finding a cheap flight simply review this book and send me an email.
philgtang@gmail.com

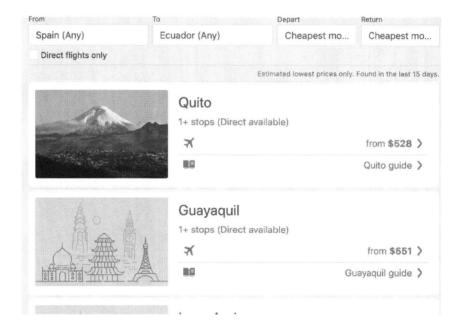

From	To	Depart	Return
Spain (Any)	Ecuador (Any)	Cheapest mo...	Cheapest mo...

Direct flights only

Estimated lowest prices only. Found in the last 15 days.

Quito
1+ stops (Direct available)

✈ from $528 >

Quito guide >

Guayaquil
1+ stops (Direct available)

✈ from $551 >

Guayaquil guide >

If you're travelling from outside Europe or the USA, I can also help you find the lowest cost direct flight. Simply review this book and email me.

Must-try Galápagos Islands Street foods

- Seafood galore. Seafood is fresh, plentiful and heavily featured on menus across the Galápagos.
- Ceviche - Galápagos's most famous dish, and for good reason: the ceviche here is divine.
- Encebollado (fish stew with lime pickles)
- Plantain (fried banana)
- Exotic fruits.
- Ice cream.

 INSIDER CULTURAL INSIGHT

Ask for the 'plata de dia'

On each island, you can go to a *local* restaurant and ask for the 'plata de dia' or plate of the day. Some advertise this with a bulletin board or written on paper. This is usually your choice of chicken/beef/fish with rice and beans and juice. On Santa Cruz it was $3 and included only a drink. On Isabella it was $5 and included an appetizer (chicken/pumpkin soup) and dessert (a banana or jello cup). On San Cristobal it included juice and dessert but no app and was $7.

Cheap Eats

Fill your stomach without emptying your wallet. Get a taste of the islands most authentic flavours with mains under $10.

(Download the offline map on google maps, (instructions 1. go to app 2. select offline apps in the left sidebar 3. go to the area you want to download 4. click download). Then simply type the restaurant names in to navigate, star them so you can see where the cheap eats are when you're out and about to avoid wasting your money at hyped tourist joints)

El Cafetal Galápagos
Delicious cheap Ecuadorian food.

Isla Grill
Dish of the day is a good budget option.

El Descanso Marinero
They have good healthy budget food.

Angermeyer Point
Vegetarian options. Delicious local food, kind staff, lovely view.

Café Hernán
Amazing traditional dishes with low prices.

Cesar's
Get the seafood menu of the day for $6.

Descanso del Guia
Authentic Ecuadorian Food. Fresh Fruit, scrambled eggs, plantains for $5.

El Toque De Melida
Ecuadorian place where locals eat in Puerto Villamil.

Avoid these tourist traps or scams

The only scam we heard of was taxi drivers scamming tourists - try to walk where possible, and take the bus. If you have to use a taxi always agree the fare before setting off.

Basic Phrases

Gracias, will be appreciated by servers.

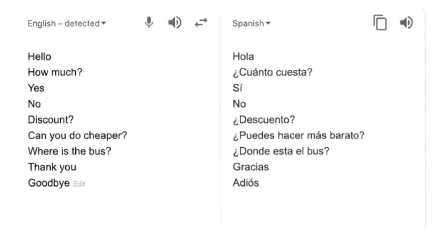

English – detected ▾	Spanish ▾
Hello	Hola
How much?	¿Cuánto cuesta?
Yes	Sí
No	No
Discount?	¿Descuento?
Can you do cheaper?	¿Puedes hacer más barato?
Where is the bus?	¿Donde esta el bus?
Thank you	Gracias
Goodbye	Adiós

Getting Out

Plane

Please note you will need to show a ticket leaving the Galápagos islands to enter, so last minute flights are not a great idea unless you find a super good deal and can justify wasting your return ticket.

At the time of writing TAME are offering the cheapest flights onwards.Take advantage of discounts and specials. Sign up for e-newsletters from local carriers including LATAM Airlines and TAME to learn about special fares. Be careful with cheap airlines, most will allow hand-luggage only, and some charge for anything that is not a backpack. Check their websites before booking if you need to take luggage.

From	To	Depart	Return
Galapagos Is (GPS)	Everywhere	Cheapest mo...	(One Way)
Direct flights only			

Estimated lowest prices only. Found in the last 15 days.

Ecuador	from $108	⌄
Colombia	from $438	⌄
Panama	from $445	⌄
United States	from $460	⌄
Peru	from $486	⌄
Germany	from $490	⌄

Personal Cost Break-down

	How	Cost normally / advice	Cost when following suggested tip
How I got from the airport	Taxi	$25 Taxi	$25
Where I stayed	Hostel or airbnb $15 a night	Hotels are upwards of $80 a night.	$45
Tastiest street foods I ate and cost	Encebollado - fish stew	Expect to pay $1 - $5 for street eats	$5
How I got around	Walk or taxi, and use ferries	Getting around is costly. Even bikes and scooters at upwards of $20 per day. Walk where you can to keep costs down.	$100
What I saw and paid	iganuas, wildlife, turtles, birds, beaches - day cruise to outer islands. entry fee	Find a cruise to get to the outer islands, its worth the money.	$170
My on-ward flight	Qutio	Book six weeks ahead for the lowest fares.	$108
My Total costs			US$400

Print or screenshot for easy reference

	How	Cost
Get from the airport	Taxi	$25
Stay	Airbnb or hostel for 3 days	$45
Food	Average meal cost: $3 – $6 - see cheap eats section.	$5 per meal
Get around	Walk and use ferries	$8 for all rides
See	Free attractions and free live music	free
Best discounts	Last minute cruise from Puerto Ayora. You can get up to 60% off the price.	$170
Get out	Quito	$108
Total	US$400	$400

PRACTICAL THINGS TO REMEMBER TO SAVE MONEY

- Book your flights to Galápagos three months ahead for the cheapest return ticket
- Download google maps for for use offline on Santa Cruz and San Cristobal
- Know the names of street foods to try and star the markets to eat at on the maps.
- Remember to ask for the plata di dia, plate of the day.
- Bring an eye-mask and earplugs if staying in hostels.
- Search for cheap last minute cruises out to Fernandina and Genovesa when you arrive. These islands is where you will see the rarest wildlife and stunning scenery. With a last-minute deal you can get a $500 experience for $250.
- Bring cash with you to pay the airport entry fees.
- Pack food for the airport, you'll save $10 on a bad cup of coffee and stale croissant at the airport.

RECAP: How to have a $1,000 trip to The Galapagos Islands on a $400 budget

Four star hotels
Book Last minute 4 star hotels deals. Check on the same day of your stay for cheap five star hotel deals. Go to booking.com enter The Galapagos Islands, tonight, only one night and filter by 5 stars. This can be very effective in the low season when hotels empty of travellers. Potential saving $800.

Eat at the markets and bakeries
If you're on a budget, but like eating out, do your eating at the markets and bakeries and opt for the plates of the day. Potential saving $100.

Go to the outer islands on the cheap
The average traveller spends $500 in The Galapagos Islands but there's no need to, if you haggle for last-minute deals to the outer islands. Potential saving $300.

Book flights early
You will need to show officials you have a return flight, so book that before you travel to save on potential price hikes, especially if you're visiting in the peak months.

The secret to saving HUGE amounts of money when travelling to the Galápagos islands is...

Your mindset. Money is an emotional topic, if you associate words like cheapskate, Miser (and its £9.50 to go into Charles Dickens London house, oh the Irony) with being thrifty when travelling you are likely to say 'F-it' and spend your money needlessly because you associate pain with saving money. You pay now for an immediate reward. Our brains are prehistoric; they focus on surviving day to day. Travel companies and hotels know this and put trillions into making you believe you will be happier when you spend on their products or services. Our poor brains are up against outdated programming and an onslaught of advertisements bombarding us with the message: spending money on travel equals PLEASURE. To correct this carefully lodged propaganda in your frontal cortex you need to imagine your future self.

Saving money does not make you a cheapskate. It makes you smart. How do people get rich? They invest their money. They don't go out and earn it; they let their money earn more money. So every time you want to spend money, imagine this: while you travel your money is working for you, not you for money. While you sleep the money you've invested is going up and up. That's a pleasure a pricey entrance fee can't give you. Thinking about putting your money to work for you tricks your brain into believing you are not withholding pleasure from yourself, you are saving your money to invest so you can go to even more amazing places. You are thus turning thrifty travel into a pleasure fueled sport.

When you've got money invested - If you want to splash your cash on a first-class airplane seat - you can. I can't tell you how to invest your money, only that you should. Saving $20 on taxi's doesn't seem like much but over time you could be saving upwards of $15,000 a year, which is a deposit for a house which you can rent on Airbnb to finance more travel. Your brain making money looks like your brain on cocaine, so tell yourself saving money is making money.

Scientists have proved that imagining your future self is the easiest way to associate pleasure with saving money. You can download FaceApp — which will give you a picture of what you will look like older and greyer, or you can take a deep breath just before spending money and ask yourself if you will regret the purchase later.

The easiest ways to waste money travelling are:

Getting a taxi. The solution to this is to always download the google map before you go. Many taxi drivers will drive you around for 15 minutes when the place you were trying to get to is a 5-minute walk... remember while not getting an overpriced taxi to tell yourself, 'I am saving money to free myself for more travel.'
Spending money on overpriced food when hungry. The solution: carry snacks. A banana and an apple will cost you, in most places less than a dollar.
Spending on entrance fees to top-rated attractions. If you really want to do it, spend the money happily. If you're conflicted sleep on it. I don't regret spending $200 on a skydive over the Great Barrier Reef, I do regret going to the top of the shard in London for $60. Only you can know but make sure it's your decision and not the marketing directors at said top-rated attraction.
Telling yourself 'you only have the chance to see/eat/experience it now'. While this might be true, make sure YOU WANT to spend the money. Money spent is money you can't invest, and often you can have the same experience for much less.

You can experience luxurious travel on a small budget which will trick your brain into thinking you're already a high-roller, which will mean you'll be more likely to start acting like one and invest your money. Stay in five-star hotels for $5 by booking on the day of your stay on booking.com to enjoy last minute deals. You can go to fancy restaurants using daily deal sites. Ask your airline about last minute upgrades to first-class or business. I paid $100 extra on a $179 ticket to Cuba from Germany to be bumped to Business Class. When you ask you will be surprised what you can get both at hotels and airlines.

Travel, as the saying goes is the only thing you spend money on that makes you richer. In practice, you can easily waste money, making it difficult to enjoy that metaphysical wealth. The biggest money saving secret is to turn bargain hunting into a pleasurable activity, not an annoyance. Budgeting consciously can be fun, don't feel disappointed because you don't spend the $60 to go into an attraction, feel good because soon that $60 will soon be earning money for you. Meaning you'll the time and money to enjoy more metaphysical wealth, while your bank balance increases.

So there it is, you can save a small fortune by being strategic with your trip planning. We've arranged everything in the guide to offer the best bang for your buck. Which means we took the view that if it's not a good investment for your money, we wouldn't include it. Why would a guide called 'Super Cheap' include lots of overpriced attractions? That said if you think we've missed something or have unanswered questions ping me an email philgtang@gmail.com I'm on central Europe time and usually reply within 8 hours of getting your mail.

Don't put your dreams off!

Time is a currency you never get back and travel is its greatest return on investment. Plus now you know you can visit The Galápagos Islands for a fraction of the price most would have you believe. Go and create unforgettable memories.

Map

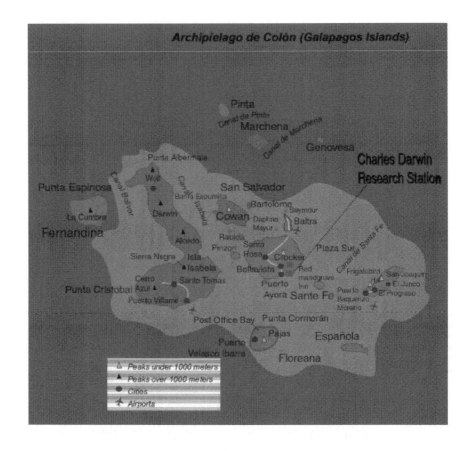

Thank you for reading

Dear Lovely Reader,

If you have found this book useful, please consider writing a short review on Amazon.

One person from every 1000 readers leaves a review on Amazon. It would mean more than you could ever know if you were one of our 1 in 1000 people to take the time to write a short review.

We are a group of four friends who all met travelling 15 years ago. We believe that great experiences don't need to blow your budget, just your mind.

Thank you so much for reading again and for spending your time and investing your trips future in Super Cheap Insider Guides.

One last note, please don't listen to anyone who says 'Oh no, you can't visit Galapagos on a budget'. Unlike you they didn't have this book. The truth is you can do ANYWHERE on a budget with the right insider advice and planning. Sure, learning to travel to Galapagos on a budget that doesn't compromise on anything or drastically compromise on safety or comfort levels is a skill, but this guide has done the detective work for you. Now it is time for you to put the advice into action.

Phil

P.S If you need any more super cheap tips we'd love to hear from you e-mail me at philgtang@gmail.com, we have a lot of contacts in every region, so if there's a specific bargain you're hunting we can help you find it :-)

SHOP 150 VACATIONS UNDER $150.

INCLUDING LONDON.

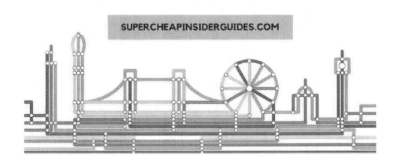

SUPERCHEAPINSIDERGUIDES.COM

Bonus Budget Travel Hacks

I've included these bonus travel hacks to help you plan and enjoy your trip to Galapagos cheaply, joyfully and smoothly. Perhaps they will even inspire you or renew your passion for long-term travel.

From saving space in your pack to scoring cheap flights, there are a wealth of generic travel hacks to help you enjoy stress-free, happier travels without breaking the bank. This is why I've included this bonus section to maximise the value you get from buying this book.

When I tell people I write a travel guide series focused on luxurious budget travel, they wrongly assume that's impossible and often say 'Hitchhiking and couch-surfing?'. Others with more vivid imaginations ask me if I recommend hooking up with older men or women… Of course, they are surprised when I tell them that not one of the 150 Super Cheap Guides endorses such practises because they maximise discomfort. They look at me dumbfounded and ask 'How on earth do you travel comfortably on a budget then?'

Travelling cheaply in a way that doesn't compromise enjoyment, comfort or safety is a skill I have honed over 20 years of travelling. My foremost learning was that locals always know the tricks and tips to enjoy the same or a better tourist experience for a 10th of the cost, and that's why I teamed up with locals in each locale to distil the tips that will save you a fortune without compromising on enjoyment or comfort.

Enjoyable budget travel is about balancing and prioritising what is important to you.
When I tell people about my methodology I often receive long defensive monologues about why they spend so much on travel, or why they can't or don't travel. Thats why we will first discuss how you can find the freedom to travel.

How to find the freedom to travel

Freedom is one of those words that can mean different things to different people. It's important to be clear on what it looks like to you in your life, and all the stories and beliefs that prevent you from having it. For me, freedom means always having at choice in my life. I don't do anything that I don't want to do. —LEO BABAUTA

We've spoken a lot about how to save money travelling to Galapagos, but how do you find the freedom if you have:

1. Pets
2. Kids
3. A spouse who doesn't want you to travel
4. A job that keeps you at home?

Like everything, there's a solution to every problem. In this chapter, I want to you to think about whether your excuses can be overcome using the following solutions, because as Randy Komisar said: "And then there is the most dangerous risk of all – the risk of spending your life not doing what you want on the bet you can buy yourself the freedom to do it later."

Pets

I have a dog, an extremely loving German Shepherd. And when I travel overland from Austria she comes with me and my wife. If we are heading on a longer trip we either leave her with friends or family or we get someone to house sit for us. housesitters.-com offers up people who are vetted and reviewed and in exchange for free accommodation will care for your pets. Just be aware it often works out financially better to rent your space on Airbnb and pay someone to look after your pets. Make sure you visit their facilities before you entrust your pet to anyone and of course, always read the reviews.

I know a lot of people miss their pets travelling which is why we endeavour to take our dog with us. Exploring with her has formed some of our most precious memories. If you're flying with your pet always look up the rules and make sure you comply. If you're going to the UK for example, they quarantine dogs who come in by air. So we only take our dog by car. Coming into the UK by car, dogs must need to be chipped, have a note from a vet saying they are clear of Rabies and tapeworms, have a pet passport and be on a course of medication for tapeworms 2 days before they enter. The UK is the strictest country I've encountered when it comes to travelling with pets so I use this as barometer. My point is, do your homework if you're bringing your furry friend, both about entry conditions and the local environment for your pet. For instance, in India, many domesticated dogs are attacked by street dogs. Educate yourself on your options and limitations but don't think because you have pets that travel is out of the question.

Kids

I also have a daughter who is about to turn 1. We have travelled to seven countries with her so far, with many more in the pipeline. The easiest way to travel with kids is in an RV. You don't have to worry about checking vast amounts of baggage or travelling with a stroller. You have unlimited freedom and can camp for free in many places. You can normally take the RV on a slow ship cheaper than the price of a plane ticket for 3 people.

A study by Cornell University found that we get more happiness from anticipating a travel experience in comparison to anticipating buying a new possession, so in that way, money can buy you happiness. If you invest in an RV, you can also turn it into a profit centre by renting it out on platforms like www.outdoorsy.com.

You don't necessarily have to fly to travel with kids, train, bus and RV's are better options. Kids become more adaptable and flexible when the world is their classroom. This is true at any age. but when kids immerse themselves in new places and engage with local cultures; this open-mindedness helps them in all aspects of their lives. For school-age children, you are limited to holiday dates, but with 12 weeks off a year, you can still find adventure together.

A spouse who doesn't want you to travel

A loving partner should always want what's best for you. Scientifically, travelling is proven to reduce stress. A study in 2000 study found that men and women who do not take a trip for several years are 30 per cent more likely to have a heart attack. It makes sense because when you travel you are more active; travellers often walk ten miles a day, sightseeing and soaking up new sights and smells.

Travelling also strengthens the 'openness' aspect of your personality and makes you less emotionally reactive to day-to-day changes, improving emotional stability. Sure, losing your baggage or almost missing a connecting flight can be panic-inducing, but, overall, the data supports that travelling is beneficial for you. Tell your partner about these studies, if they don't want a healthier, happier, more emotionally stable you, then it may be time to consider why you're investing your time with this person.

Another common issue is mismatched travel budgets. If you and your partner travel together and they force you to overspend with the 'we're on holiday/vacation!' appendage, here's a tip from one of our writers Kim:

'My husband and I were always having 'discussions' about money during our trips. I love bargains and he is the kind of traveller who's totally cool to be ripped off because he normally travels for business and has become used to spending corporate money. The compromise we reached is that he reads a shoestring or super cheap guide before the trip. Then when he wants to waste money, I say yes, but only in exchange for doing one budget item from the guide. It has worked wonders, lessened our 'discussions' and he now actually chooses cheaper destinations as he sees budgeting as a game.'

A job that keeps you at home

Our lives can feel constantly busy. Sometimes we may feel we are sinking beneath our workload. If you're close to or suffering a burnout the stress relief that comes from novelty and change in the form of new people, sights and experiences is the best remedy you could give to yourself.

If you're in a job that is hurting your health or well-being its time to reconsider why. It is often the case that you believe the work to be deeply rewarding, but if that reward leaves you ill, uninspired and fatigued, you can't help anyone. I learnt this the hard way when I worked for a charity whose mission I deeply resonated with. After 3 years of 70 hour work weeks, I'd lost hair, teeth, direction and, if I'm honest, faith in humanity. It took me 3 years to come back to the light and see that I chose a very stressful job that my body told me repeatedly it could not handle. Travel was a big part of forgiving myself. It helped me put old stories that held me back and probably sent me into this quagmire of self-abuse via work into perspective.

Sometimes we keep letting ourselves make excuses about why we're not travelling because we're scared of the unknown. In such cases, one of three things happens that forces a person from their nest:

- A traumatic event
- Completing a major milestone
- A sudden realisation or epiphany

Do yourself a favour, don't wait for any of those. Decide you want to travel, and book a flight. Our next section takes you through how to book the cheapest possible flight.

HOW TO FIND CHEAP FLIGHTS

"The use of travelling is to regulate imagination by reality, and instead of thinking how things may be, to see them as they are." S amuel Jackson

If you're working full-time you can save yourself a lot of money

by requesting your time off from work starting in the middle of the week. Tuesdays and Wednesdays are the cheapest days to fly, you can save hundreds just by adjusting your time off.

The simplest secret to booking cheap flights is open parameters. Let's say you want to fly from Chicago to Paris. You

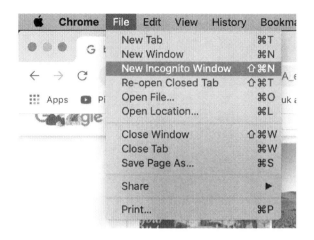

need to enter USA to France, you may find flights from NYC to Paris for $70 and can take a cheap flight to NYC. Make sure you calculate full costs, including if you need airport accommodation and of course getting to and from airports, but in every instance open parameters will save you at least half the cost of the flight.

If you're not sure about where you want to go, use open parameters to show you the cheapest destinations from your city.
Use skyscanner.net - they include the low-cost airlines that others like Kayak leave out.

Open parameters can also show you the cheapest dates to fly. If you're flexible you can save up to 80% of the flight cost. Always check the weather at your destination before you book, sometimes a $400 flight will be $20, because its monsoon season. But hey, if you like the rain, why not?

ALWAYS USE A PRIVATE BROWSER TO BOOK FLIGHTS

Skyscanner and other sites track your IP address and put prices up and down based on what they determine your strength of conviction to buy. e.g if you've booked one-way and are looking for the return these sites will jack the prices up by in most cases 50%. Incognito browsing pays.

Use a VPN such as Hola to book your flight from your destination

Install Hola, change your destination to the country you are flying to. The location from which a ticket is booked can affect the price significantly as algorithms take into account local buying power.

Choose the right time to buy your ticket.

Choose the right time to buy your ticket, as purchasing tickets on a Sunday has been proven to be cheaper. If you can only book during the week, try to do it on a Tuesday.

Mistake fares

Email alerts from individual carriers are where you can find the best 'mistake fares". This is where a computer error has resulted in an airline offering the wrong fare. In my experience its best to sign up to individual carriers email lists but if you ARE lazy Secret Flying puts together a daily roster of mistake fares. Visit
                                    to see if there's any errors that can benefit you.

Fly late for cheaper prices.

Red-eye flights, the ones that leave later in the day, are typically cheaper and less crowded, so aim to book that flight if possible. You will also get through the airport much quicker at the end of the day, just make sure there's ground transport available for when you land. You don't want to save $50 on the airfare and spend it on a taxi to your accommodation.

Use this APP for same day flights

If you're plans are flexible, use 'Get The Flight Out' (
) a fare tracker Hopper that shows you
same-day deeply discounted flights. This is best for long-
haul flights with major carriers. You can often find a British
Airways round-trip from JFK Airport to Heathrow for $300. If
you booked this in advance you'd pay at least double.

Take an empty water bottle with you

Airport prices on food and drinks are sky-high. It disgusts
me to see some airports charging $10 for a bottle of water.
ALWAYS take an empty water bottle with you. It's relatively
unknown, but most airports have drinking water fountains
past the security check. Just type in your airport name to
                    to locate the fountain. Then once
you've passed security (because they don't allow you to
take 100ml or more of liquids) you can freely refill your bottle with water.

Round-the-World (RTW) Tickets

It is always cheaper to book your flights using a DIY approach.
First, you may decide you want to stay longer in one country,
and a RTW will charge you a hefty fee for changing your flight.
Secondly, it all depends on where and when you travel and as
we have discussed, there are many ways to ensure you pay way
less than $1,500 for a year of flights. If you're travelling long-
haul, the best strategy is to buy a return ticket, say New York to
Bangkok and then take cheap flights or transport around Asia
and even to Australia and beyond.

Frequent Flyer Memberships

A frequent-flyer program (FFP) is a loyalty program offered by an airline. They are designed to encourage airline customers to fly more to accumulate points (also called miles, kilometres, or segments) which can be redeemed for air travel or other rewards.

You can sign up with any FFP program for free. There are three major airline alliances in the world: Oneworld, SkyTeam and Star Alliance. I am with One World https://www.oneworld.com/members because the points can be accrued and used for most flights.

The best return on your points is to use them for international business or first class flights with lie-flat seats. You would need 3 times more miles compared to an economy flight, but if you paid cash, you'd pay 5 - 10 times more than the cost of the economy flight, so it really pays to use your points only for upgrades. The worst value for your miles is to buy an economy seat or worse, a gift from the airlines gift-shop.

Sign up for a family/household account to pool miles together. If you share a common address you can claim the miles with most airlines. You can use AwardWallet to keep track of your miles. Remember that they only last for 2 years, so use them before they expire.

Pack like a Pro

"He who would travel happily must travel light." – Antoine de St. Exupery 59.

Travel as lightly as you can. We always need less than we think. You will be very grateful that you have a light pack when changing trains, travelling through the airport, catching a bus, walking to your accommodation, or climbing stairs.

Make a list of what you will wear for 7 days and take only those clothes. You can easily wash your things while you're travelling if you stay in an Airbnb with a washing machine or visit a local laundrette. Roll your clothes for maximum space usage and fewer wrinkles. If you feel really nervous about travelling with such few things make sure you have a dressier outfit, a little black dress for women is always valuable, a shirt for men. Then pack shorts, long pair of pants, loose tops and a hoodie to snuggle in. Remind yourself that a lack of clothing options is an opportunity to find bargain new outfits in thrift stores. You can either sell these on eBay after you've worn them or post them home to yourself. You'll feel less stressed, as you don't have to look after or feel weighed down by excess baggage. Here are three things to remember when packing:

- Co-ordinate colours - make sure everything you bring can be worn together.
- Be happy to do laundry - fresh clothes when you're travelling feels very luxurious.
- Take liquid minis no bigger than 60ml. Liquid is heavy and you simply don't need to carry so much at one time.

Checks to Avoid Fees

Always have 6 months validity on your passport

To enter most countries you need 6 months from the day you land. Factor in different time zones around the world if your passport is on the edge. Airport security will stop you from boarding your flight at the airport if your passport has 5 months and 29 days left.

Google Your Flight Number before you leave for the airport

Easily find out where your plane is from anywhere. Confirm the status of your flight before you leave for the airport with flightaware.com. This can save you long unnecessary wait times.

Check-in online

The founder, Ryan O'Leary of budget airline RyanAir famously said: "We think they should pay €60 for [failing to check-in on-line] being so stupid.". Always check-in online, even for international flights. Cheaper international carriers like Scoot will charge you at the airport to check-in.

Checking Bags

Never, ever check a bag if you possibly can avoid it. It is always cheaper to put heavier items on a ship, rather than take them on a flight with you. Find the best prices for shipping at https://www.parcelmonkey.com/delivery-services/shipping-heavy-items

Use a fragile sticker

Put a 'Fragile' sticker on anything you check to ensure that it's handled better as it goes through security. It'll also be one of the first bags released after the flight, getting you out of the airport quicker.

If you do check your bag, photograph it

Take a photo of your bag before you check it. This will speed up the paperwork if it is damaged or lost.

Relaxing at the airport

The best way to relax at the airport is in a lounge where they provide free food, drinks, comfortable chairs, luxurious amenities (many have showers) and if you're lucky a peaceful ambience. If you're there for a longer time look for Airport Cubicles, sleep pods which charge by the hour.

You can use your FFP Card (Frequent Flyer Memberships) to get into select lounges for free. Check your eligibility before you pay.

If you're travelling a lot I'd recommend to Invest in a Priority Pass for the airport.
It includes 850-plus airport lounges around the world. The cost is $99 for the year and $27 per lounge visit or you can pay $399 for the year all inclusive.

If you need a lounge for a one-off day, you can get a Day Pass. Buy it online for a discount, it always works out cheaper than buying at the airport. Use   .

Lounges are also great if you're travelling with kids, as they're normally free for kids and will definitely cost you less than snacks for your little ones. The rule is that kids should be seen and not heard, so consider this before taking an overly excited child who wants to run around, or you might be asked to leave even after you've paid.

Money: How to make it, spend it and save it while travelling

How to earn money WHILE travelling

"Twenty years from now you will be more disappointed by the things you didn't do than by the ones you did do. So throw off the bowlines. Sail away from the safe harbour." - H. Jackson Brown

Digital nomads receive a lot of hype. Put simply they are "professionals who work online and therefore don't need to tie themselves to one particular office, city, or even country."

The first step in becoming a digital nomad, earning money while travelling is knowing what you can offer. Your market is the whole world. So, what product or service would you like to offer that they would pay for? Take some time to think about this. In German, they say you should do whatever comes easily to your hand. For example, I've always loved finding bargains, it comes very easily for me. Yet I studied Law and Finance at University, which definitely did not come easy. It's no shock that it didn't transpire into a career. And served more as a lesson in not following my ego.

There are thousands of possibilities to generate income while travelling; offering services like tutorial, coaching, writing service pr blogging. Most travellers I meet try their hand at blogging and earning from the advertisements. This is great if you have some savings, but if you need to earn straight away to travel, this should be on the back burner, as it takes time to establish. Still if this comes easily to you, do it!

You want to make good money fast. Ask yourself, what is it that you are good at and how can you deliver maximum value to other people? Here are some ideas if you're totally dumfounded:

1. Teaching English online - you will need a private room for this. Be aware that if you're from the USA and the country you want to work in requires a federal-level background check, it

may take months, so apply early. Opportunities are on: t.vip-kid.com.cn, abc360.com, italki.com, verbalplanet.com and
. You can expect to earn $20 an hour.

2. Work in a hostel. Normally you'll get some cash and free accommodation.
3. Fruit picking. I picked Bananas in Tully Australia for $20 an hour. The jobs are menial but can be quite meditative. Look on WWOOF.org for organic farm work.
4. fiverr.com - offer a small service, like making a video template and changing the content for each buyer.
5. Do freelance work online: marketing, finance, writing, App creation, graphic designer, UX or UI designer, SEO optimizer / expert. Create a profile on upwork.com - you need to put in a lot of work to make this successful, but if you have a unique skill like coding, or marketing it can be very lucrative.
6. Make a udemy.com course. Can you offer a course in something people will pay for? e.g. stock trading, knitting or marketing.
7. Use skype to deliver all manner of services: language lessons, therapy, coaching etc. Google for what you could offer. Most specialisms have a platform you can use to find clients and they will take a cut of your earnings/ require a fee.
8. You could work on luxury yachts in the med. Its hard work, but you can save money - DesperateSailors.com
9. Become an Airbnb experience host - but this requires you to know one place and stay there for a time. And you will need a work visa for that country.
10. Work on a cruise ship. This isn't a digital nomad job but it will help you travel and save at the same time.
11. Rent your place out on airbnb while you travel and get a cleaner to manage it. The easiest solution if you own or have a long-term rent contract.

How to spend money

Budget travel hacking begins with a strategy to spend without fees. Your individual strategy depends greatly on the country you legally reside in as to what cards are available. Happily there are some fin-tech solutions which can save you thousands and are widely available globally. I will address those first:

N26
N26 is a 10-year old digital bank. I have been using them for over 6 years. The key advantage is fee-free card transactions abroad. They have a very elegant app, where you can check your timeline for all transactions listed in realtime or manage your in-app security anywhere. The card you receive is a Mastercard so you can use it everywhere. If you lose the card, you don't have to call anyone, just open the app and swipe 'lock card'. It puts your purchases into a graph automatically so you can see what you spend on. You can open an account from abroad entirely online, all you need is your passport and a camera

Revolut
Revolut is a multi-currency account that allows you to hold and exchange 29 currencies and spend fee-free abroad. It's a UK based neobank, but accepts customers from all over the world.

TransferWise debit card
If you're going to be in one place for a long time the The TransferWise debit card is like having your travel money on a card – it lets you spend money at the real exchange rate.

Monzo
Monzo is good if your UK based. They offer a fee-free UK account. Fee-free international money transfers and fee-free spending abroad.

The downside

The cards above are debit cards, meaning you need to have money in those accounts to spend it. This comes with one big downside: safety. Credit card issuers' have "zero liability" mean-

ing you're not liable for unauthorised charges. All of the cards listed above do provide cover for unauthorised charges but times vary greatly in how quickly you'd get your money back if it were stolen.

The best option is to check in your country to see which credit cards are the best for travelling and set up monthly payments to repay the whole amount so you don't pay unnecessary interest. In the USA, Schwab[1] regularly ranks at the top for travel credit cards. Credit cards are always the safer option when abroad simply because you get your money back faster if its stolen and if you're renting cars, most will give you free insurance when you book the car rental using the card, saving you money.

---

[1] Charles Schwab High Yield Checking accounts refund every single ATM fee worldwide, require no minimum balance and have no monthly fee.

Always withdraw money; never exchange.

Money exchanges whether they be on the streets or in the airports will NEVER give you a good exchange rate. Do not bring bundles of cash. Instead withdraw local currency from the ATM as needed and try to use only free ATM's. Many in airports charge you a fee to withdraw cash. Look for bigger ATM's attached to banks to avoid this.

Recap:

- Take cash from local, non-charging ATMs for the best rates.
- Never change at airport exchange desks unless you absolutely have to, then just change just enough to be able get to a bank ATM.
- Bring a spare credit card for emergencies.
- Split cash in various places on your person (pockets, shoes) and in your luggage. Its never sensible to keep your cash or cards all in one place.
- In higher risk areas, use a money belt under your clothes or put $50 in your shoe or bra.

How to save money while travelling

Saving money while travelling sounds like an oxymoron, but it can be done with little to no effort. Einstein is credited as saying, "Compound interest is the eighth wonder of the world." If you saved and invested $100 today, in 20 years it would be $2,000 thanks to the power of compound interest. It makes sense then to save your money, invest and make even more money.

The Acorns app is a simple system for this. It rounds up your credit card purchases and puts the rest into a savings account. So if you pay for a coffee and its $3.01, you'll save 0.99 cents. You won't even notice you're saving by using this app:

Here are some more generic ways you can always save money while travelling:

Device Safety
Having your phone, iPad or laptop stolen is one BIG and annoying way you can lose money traveling. The simple solution is to use apps to track your devices. Some OSes have this feature built-in. Prey will try your smartphones or laptops (preyproject.com).

Book New Airbnb's
When you take a risk on a new Airbnb listing, you save money. Just make sure the hosts profile is at least 3 years old and has reviews.

If you end up in an overcrowded city

The website   is like Airbnb for
camping in people's garden and is a great way to save
money if you end up in a city during a big event.

Look out for free classes
Lots of hostels offer free classes for guests. If you're planning to stay in a hostel, check out what classes your hostel
offers. I have learnt languages, cooking techniques, dance
styles, drawing and all manner of things for free by taking
advantage of free classes at hostels.

Get a student discount card
If you're studying buy an ISIC card - International Student
Identity Card. It is internationally recognised, valid
in 133 countries and offers more than 150,000 discounts!

Instal
Maps me is extremely good for travelling without data. It's
like offline google maps without the huge download size.

Always buy travel insurance
Don't travel without travel insurance. It is a small cost to pay
compared with what could be a huge medical bill.

How to ensure your travel insurance covers you for COVID-19

Many insurers stopped selling travel insurance after the start of
the pandemic, some have returned with some form of 'COVID-19
cover'. MoneySupermarket.com is updating a list of insurers who
cover you for varying degrees of pandemic-related travel disrup-
tion. Check on their website before buying a policy to avoid having to wade through the fine print - much of which is not written in
plain English and may contain degrees of pandemic coverage
such as they will pay your medical expenses but not your flight

home. Book hotels and flights with a credit card that cover pandemic-related travel expenses for an added level of security.

REMEMBER if you travel to a country your government is currently advising against travel to for your planned dates, then it's likely that you won't be covered at all.

Travel Apps That'll Make Budget Travel Easier

Travel apps are useful for booking and managing travel logistics. They have one fatal downside, they can track you in the app and keep prices up. If you face this, access the site from an incognito browser tab.

Here are the best apps and what they can do for you:

- Best For flight Fare-Watching: Hopper.
- Best for booking flights: Skyscanner
- Best for timing airport arrivals: FlightAware - check on delays, cancellations and gate changes.
- Best for overcoming a fear of flying: SkyGuru - turbulence forecasts for the route you're flying.
- Best for sharing your location: TripWhistle - text or send your GPS coordinates or location easily.
- Best for splitting expenses among co-travellers: Splittr, Trip Splitter, Venmo or Splitwise.

We have covered the best apps and websites for Galapagos in the section above called useful websites.

How NOT to be ripped off

"One of the great things about travel is that you find out how ma
ny good, kind people there are."
— Edith Wharton

The quote above may seem ill placed in a chapter entitled how
not to be ripped off, but I included it to remind you that the vast
majority of people do not want to rip you off. In fact, scammers
are normally limited to three situations:

1. Around heavily visited attractions - these places are targeted
   purposively due to sheer footfall. Many criminals believe rip-
   ping people off is simply a numbers game.
2. In cities or countries with low-salaries or communist ideolo-
   gies. If they can't make money in the country, they seek to
   scam foreigners. If you have travelled to India, Morocco or
   Cuba you will have observed this phenomenon.
3. When you are stuck and the person helping you knows you
   have limited options.

Scammers know that most people will avoid confrontation.
Don't feel bad about utterly ignoring someone and saying
no. Here are six strategies to avoid being ripped off:

1. **Never ever agree to pay as much as you want. Always
   decide on a price before.**
Whoever you're dealing with is trained to tell you, they are unin-
terested in money. This is a trap. If you let people do this they will
ask for MUCH MORE money at the end, and because you have
used there service, you will feel obliged to pay. This is a con-
man's trick and nothing more.

2. Pack light
You can move faster and easier. If you take heavy luggage you
will end up taking taxi's which are comparatively very costly over
time.

3. NEVER use the airport taxi service. Plan to use public transport before you reach the airport.

4. Don't buy a sim card from the airport. Buy from the local supermarkets it will cost 50% less.

5. Eat at local restaurants serving regional food
Food defines culture. Exploring all delights available to the palate doesn't need to cost huge sums.

6. Ask the locals what something should cost, and try not to pay over that.

7. If you find yourself with limited options. e.g. your taxi dumps you on the side of the road because you refuse to pay more (common in India and parts of South America) don't act desperate and negotiate as if you have other options or you will be extorted.

8. Don't blindly rely on social media

Let's say you post in a Facebook group that you want tips for travelling to The Maldives. A lot of the comments you will receive come from guides, hosts and restaurants doing their own promotion. It's estimated that 50% or more of Facebook's current monthly active users are fake[2]. And what's worse, a recent study found Social media platforms leave 95% of reported fake accounts up[3]. These accounts are the digital versions of the men who hang around the Grand Palace in Bangkok telling tourists its closed, to divert you to

---

2

3

shops where they will receive a commission for bring-ing you.

It can also be the case that genuine comments come from people who have totally different interests, beliefs and yes, budgets to yours. Make your experience your own and don't believe every comment you read.

Bottom line: use caution when accepting recommenda-tions on social <u>media</u> and always fact-check with your own research.

Small tweaks on the road add up to big differences in your bank balance

Take advantage of other hotel's amenities

If you fancy a swim but you're nowhere near the ocean, try the nearest hotel with a pool. As long as you buy a drink, the hotel staff will likely grant you access.

Fill up your mini bar for free.

Fill up your mini bar for free by storing things from the breakfast bar or grocery shop in your mini bar to give you a greater selection of drinks and food without the hefty price tag.

Save yourself some ironing

Use the steam from the shower to get rid of wrinkles in clothing. If something is creased, leave it trapped with the steam in the bathroom overnight for even better results.

See somewhere else for free

Opt for long stopovers, allowing you to experience another city without spending much money.

Wear your heaviest clothes

on the plane to save weight in your pack, allowing you to bring more with you. Big coats can then be used as pillows to make your flight more comfortable.

Don't get lost while you're away.

Find where you want to go using Google Maps, then type 'OK Maps' into the search bar to store this information for offline viewing.

Use car renting services

Share Now or Car2Go allow you to hire a car for 2 hours for $25 in a lot of Europe.

Share Rides

Use sites like blablacar.com to find others who are driving in your direction. It can be 80% cheaper than normal transport. Just check the drivers reviews.

Use free gym passes

Get a free gym day pass by googling the name of a local gym and free day pass.

When asked by people providing you a service where you are from..

If there's no price list for the service you are asking for, when asked where you are from, Say you are from a lesser-known poorer country. I normally say Macedonia, and if they don't know where it is, add it's a poor country. If you say UK, USA, the majority of Europe bar the well-known poorer countries taxi drivers, tour operators etc will match the price to what they think you pay at home.

Set-up a New Uber/ other car hailing app account for discounts

By googling you can find offers with $50 free for new users in most cities for Uber/ Lyft/ Bolt and alike. Just set up a new gmail.com email account to take advantage.

Where and How to Make Friends

"People don't take trips, trips take people." – John Steinbeck

Become popular at the airport

Want to become popular at the airport? Pack a power bar with multiple outlets and just see how many friends you can make. It's amazing how many people forget their chargers, or who packed them in the luggage that they checked in.

Stay in Hostels

First of all, Hostels don't have to be shared dorms, and they cater to a much wider demographic than is assumed. Hostels are a better environment for meeting people than hotels, and more importantly they tended to open up excursion opportunities that further opened up that opportunity.

Or take up a hobby

If hostels are a definite no-no for you; find an interest. Take up a hobby where you will meet people. I've dived for years and the nature of diving is you're always paired up with a dive buddy. I met a lot of interesting people that way.

When unpleasantries come your way...

We all have our good and bad days travelling, and on a bad day you can feel like just taking a flight home. Here are some ways to overcome common travel problems:

Anxiety when flying

It has been over 40 years since a plane has been brought down by turbulence. Repeat that number to yourself: 40 years! Planes are built to withstand lighting strikes, extreme storms and ultimately can adjust course to get out of their way. Landing and take off are when the most accidents happen, but you have statistically three times the chance of winning a huge jackpot lottery, then you do of dying in a plane crash.

If you feel afraid on the flight focus on your breathing saying the word 'smooth' over and over until the flight is smooth. Always check the airline safety record on airlinerating.com I was surprised to learn Ryanair and Easyjet as much less safe than Wizz Air according to those ratings because they sell similarly priced flights. If there is extreme turbulence, I feel much better knowing I'm in a 7 star safety plane.

Wanting to sleep instead of seeing new places

This is a common problem. Just relax, there's little point doing fun things when you feel tired. Factor in jet-lag to your travel plans. When you're rested and alert you'll enjoy your new temporary home much more. Many people hate the first week of a long-trip because of jet-lag and often blame this on their first destination, but its rarely true. Ask travellers who 'hate' a particular place and you will see, that very often they either had jet-lag or an unpleasant journey there.

Going over budget

Come back from a trip to a monster credit card bill? Hopefully this guide has prevented you from returning to an unwanted bill. Of course, there are costs that can creep up and this is a reminder about how to prevent them making their way on to your credit card bill:

- To and from the airport. Solution: leave adequate time and take the cheapest method - book before.
- Baggage. Solution: take hand luggage and post things you might need to yourself.
- Eating out. Solution: go to cheap eats places and suggest those to friends.
- Parking. Solution: use apps to find free parking
- Tipping. Solution Leave a modest tip and tell the server you will write them a nice review.
- Souvenirs. Solution: fridge magnets only.
- Giving to the poor. (This one still gets me, but if you're giving away $10 a day - it adds up) Solution: volunteer your time instead and recognise that in tourist destinations many beggars are run by organised crime gangs.

Price v Comfort

I love traveling, I don't love struggling. I like decent accommodation, being able to eat properly and see places and enjoy. I am never in the mood for low cost airlines or crappy transfers so here's what I do to save money.

- Avoid organised tours unless you are going to a place where safety is a real issue. They are expensive and constrain your wanderlust to typical things. I only recommend them in Algeria, Iran and Papua New Guinea - where language and gender views pose serious problems all cured by a reputable tour organiser.
- Eat what the locals do.
- Cook in your airbnb/ hostel where restaurants are expensive.
- Shop at local markets.
- Spend time choosing your flight, and check the operator on arilineratings.com
- Mix up hostels and Airbnbs. Hostels for meeting people, Airbnb for relaxing and feeling 'at home'.

Not knowing where free toilets are

Use Toilet Finder - https://play.google.com/store/apps/details?id=com.bto.toilet&hl=en

Your airbnb is awful

Airbnb customer service is notoriously bad. Help yourself out. Try to sort things out with the host, but if you can't, take photos of everything e.g bed, bathroom, mess, doors, contact them within 24 hours. Tell them you had to leave and pay for new accommodation. Ask politely for a full refund including booking fees. With photographic evidence and your new accommodation receipt, they can't refuse.

The airline loses your bag

Go to the Luggage desk before leaving the airport and report the bag missing.
Most airlines will give you an overnight bag, ask where your staying and return the bag to you within three days. Its extremely rare for them to completely lose it due to technological innovation, but if that happens you should submit an insurance claim after the

three days is up, including receipts for everything your had to buy in the interim.

Your travel companion lets you down.

Whether it's a breakup or a friend cancelling, it sucks and can ramp up costs. The easiest solution to finding a new travel companion is to go to a well-reviewed hostel and find someone you want to travel with. You should spend at least three days getting to know this person before you suggest travelling together. Finding someone in person is always better than finding someone online, because you can get a better idea of whether you will have a smooth journey together. Travel can make or break friendships.

Culture shock

I had one of the strongest culture shocks while spending 6 months in Japan. It was overwhelming how much I had to prepare when I went outside of the door (googling words and sentences what to use, where to go, which station and train line to use, what is this food called in Japanese and how does its look etc.). I was so tired constantly but in the end I just let go and went with my extremely bad Japanese. If you feel culture shocked its because your brain is referencing your surroundings to what you know. Stop comparing, have Google translate downloaded and relax.

Your Car rental insurance is crazy expensive

I always use carrentals.com and book with a credit card. Most credit cards will give you free insurance for the car, so you don't need to pay the extra.

You're sick

First off ALWAYS, purchase travel insurance. Including emergency transport up to $500k even to back home, which is usually less than $10 additional. I use https://www.comparethemarket.com/travel-insurance/ to find the best days. If I am sick I normally check into a hotel with room service and ride it out.

Make a Medication Travel Kit

Take travel sized medications with you:

- Antidiarrheal medication (for example, bismuth subsalicylate, loperamide)
- Medicine for pain or fever (such as acetaminophen, aspirin, or ibuprofen)
- Throat Lozenges

Save yourself from most travel related hassles

- Do not make jokes with immigration and customs staff. A misunderstanding can lead to HUGE fines.

- Book the most direct flight you can find, nonstop if possible.

- Carry a US$50 bill for emergency cash. I have entered a country and all ATM and credit card systems were down. US$ can be exchanged nearly anywhere in the world and is useful in extreme situations, but where possible don't exchange, as you will lose money.

- Check, and recheck, required visas and such BEFORE the day of your trip. Some countries, for instance, require a ticket out of the country in order to enter. Others, like the

US and Australia, require electronic authorisation in advance.

- Airport security is asinine and inconsistent around the world. Keep this in mind when connecting flights. Always leave at least 2 hours for international connections or international to domestic. In London Stansted for example, they force you to buy one of their plastic bags, and remove your liquids from your own plastic bag.... just to make money from you. And this adds to the time it will take to get through security so lines are long.

- Wiki travel is perfect to use for a lay of the land.

- Expensive luggage rarely lasts longer than cheap luggage, in my experience. Fancy leather bags are toast with air travel.
-

Food

- When it comes to food, eat in local restaurants, not tourist-geared joints. Any place with the menu in three or more languages is going to be overpriced.
- Take a spork - a knife, spoon and fork all in one.

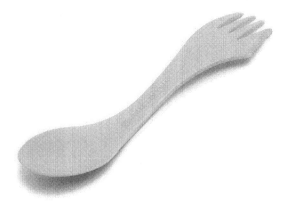

Water Bottle

Take a water bottle with a filter. We love these ones from Water to Go.
Empty it before airport security and separate the bottle and filter as some airport people will try and claim it has liquids…

Bug Sprays

If you're heading somewhere tropical spray your clothes with Permethrin before you travel. It lasts 40 washes and saves space in your bag. A 'Bite Away' zapper can be used after the bite to totally erase it. It cuts down on the itching and erases the bite from your skin.

Order free mini's

Don't buy those expensive travel sized toiletries, order travel sized freebies online. This gives you the opportunity to try brands you've never used before, and who knows, you might even find your new favourite soap.

Take a waterproof bag

If you're travelling alone you can swim without worrying about your phone, wallet and passport laying on the beach. You can also use it as a source of entertainment on those ultra budget flights.

Make a private entertainment centre anywhere

Always take an eye-mask, earplugs, a scarf and a kindle reader - so you can sleep and entertain yourself anywhere!

The best Travel Gadgets

The door alarm

If you're nervous and staying in private rooms or airbnbs take a door alarm. For those times when you just don't feel safe, it can help you fall asleep. You can get tiny ones for less than $10 from Amazon:

Smart Blanket

Amazon sells a 6 in 1 heating blanket that is very useful for cold plane or bus trips. Its great if you have poor circulation as it becomes a detachable Foot Warmer: Amazon http://amzn.to/2hTYlOP I paid $49.00.

The coat that becomes a tent

https://www.adiff.com/products/tent-jacket. This is great if you're going to be doing a lot of camping.

Clever Tank Top with Secret Pockets

Keep your valuables safe in this top. Perfect for all climates.

on Amazon for $39.90

Optical Camera Lens for Smartphones and Tablets
Leave your bulky camera at home. Turn your device into a high-performance camera. Buy on Amazon for $9.95

Travel-sized Wireless Router with USB Media Storage

Convert any wired network to a wireless network. Buy on Amazon for $17.99

Buy a Scrubba Bag to wash your clothes on the go
Or a cheaper imitable. You can wash your clothes on the go.

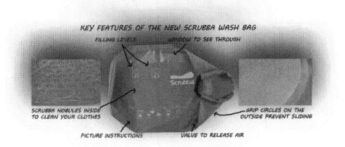

Hacks for Families

Rent an Airbnb apartment so you can cook

Apartments are much better for families, as you have all the amenities you'd have at home. They are normally cheaper per person too. We are the first travel guide publisher to include Airbnb's in our recommendations if you think any of these need updating you can email me at philgtang@gmail.com

Shop at local markets

Eat seasonal products and local products. Get closer to the local market and observe the prices and the offer. What you can find more easily, will be the cheapest

Take Free Tours

Download free podcast tours of the destination you are visiting. The podcast will tell you where to start, where to go, and what to look for. Often you can find multiple podcast tours of the same place. Listen to all of them if you like, each one will tell you a little something new.

Pack Extra Ear Phones

If you go on a museum tour, they often have audio guides. Instead of having to rent one for each person, take some extra earphones. Most audio tour devices have a place to plug in a second set.

Buy Souvenirs Ahead of Time

If you are buying souvenirs someone touristy, you are paying a premium price. By ordering the same exact products online, you can save a lot of money.

Use Cheap Transportation

Do as the locals do, including weekly passes.

Carry Reusable Water Bottles

Spending money on water and other beverages can quickly add up. Instead of paying for drinks, take some refillable water bottles.

Combine Attractions

Many major cities offer ticket bundles where one price gets you into 5 or 6 popular attractions. You will need to plan ahead of time to decide what things you plan to do on vacation and see if they are selling these activities together.

Pack Snacks

Granola bars, apples, baby carrots, bananas, cheese crackers, juice boxes, pretzels, fruit snacks, apple sauce, grapes, and veggie chips.

Stick to Carry-On Bags

Do not pay to check a large bag. Even a small child can pull a carry-on.

Visit free art galleries and museums

Just google the name + free days.

Eat Street Food

There's a lot of unnecessary fear around this. You can watch the food prepared. Go for the stands that have a steady queue.

Travel Gadgets for Families

Dropcam

Are what-if scenarios playing out in your head? Then you need Dropcam.

'Dropcam HD Internet Wi-Fi Video Monitoring Cameras help you watch what you love from anywhere. In less than a minute, you'll have it setup and securely streaming video to you over your home Wi-Fi. Watch what you love while away with Dropcam HD.'

Approximate Price: $139

Kelty-Child-Carrier

Voted as one of the best hiking essentials if you're traveling with kids and can carry a child up to 18kg.

Jetkids Bedbox

No more giving up your own personal space on the plane with this suitcase that becomes a bed.

Safety

"If you think adventure is dangerous, try routine. It's lethal." – Paulo Coelho

Backpacker murdered is a media headline that leads people to think traveling is more dangerous than it is. The media sensationalise the rare murders and deaths of backpackers and travellers. The actual chances of you dying abroad are extremely extremely low.

Let's take the USA as an example. In 2018, 724 Americans **died** from unnatural causes, 167 died from car accidents, while the majority of the other deaths resulted from drownings, suicides, and non-vehicular accidents. Contrast this with the 15,000 murders in the US in 2018, and travelling abroad looks much safer than staying at home.

There are many thing you can to keep yourself save. Here are out tips.

1. Always check fco.co.uk before travelling. NEVER RELY on websites or books. Things are changing constantly and the FCO's (UK's foreign office) advice is always UP TO DATE (hourly) and extremely conservative.
2. Check your mindset. I've travelled alone to over 180 countries and the main thing I learnt is if you walk around scared, or anticipating you're going to be pickpocketed, your constant fear will attract bad energy. Murders or attacks on travellers are the mainstay of media, not reality, especially in countries familiar with travellers. The only place I had cause to genuinely fear for my life was Papa New Guinea - where nothing actually happened to me only my own panic over culture shock.

There are many things you can do to stop yourself being victim to the two main problems when travelling: theft or being scammed.

I will address theft first. Here are my top tips:

- Stay alert while you're out and always have an exit strategy.
- Keep your money in a few different places on your person and your passport somewhere it can't be grabbed.
- Take a photo of your passport on your phone incase. If you do lose it, google for your embassy, you can usually get a temporary pretty fast.
- Google safety tips for traveling in your country to help yourself out and memorise the emergency number.
- At hostels keep your large bag in the room far under the bed/ out of the way with a lock on the zipper.
- On buses/trains I would even lock my bag to the luggage rack.
- Get a personal keychain alarm. The sound will scare anyone away.
- Don't wear any jewellery. A man attempted to rob a friend of her engagement ring in Bogota, Colombia, and in hindsight I wished I'd told her to leave it at home/wear it on a hidden necklace, as the chaos it created was avoidable.
- Don't turn your back to traffic while you use your phone.
- When traveling in the tuktuk sit in the middle and keep your bag secure. Wear sunglasses as dust can easily get in your eyes.
- Don't let anyone give you flowers, bracelets, or any type of trinket, even if they insist it's for free and compliment you like crazy.
- Don't let strangers know that you are alone - unless they are travel friends ;-)
- Lastly, and most importantly -Trust your gut! If it doesn't feel right, it isn't.

Hilarious Travel Stories

I have compiled these short stories from fellow travellers to pick you up when you're feeling down. Life on the road isn't always easy and we've all had those days when we want to stay in bed and forget the world exists. Laughter is the best way I know to shake those feelings. All people who have shared these stories wanted to remain anonymous. After reading them I think you'll understand why...

I mentioned my wife earlier, so its only fair she be the first story. Don't worry she has given me permission to share.

A marriage up the wall

'Delhi belly got me on the third day into the trip to India. I was vomiting so much that I couldn't keep even water down so I went to a health clinic for tourists. Whilst I was there I was asked to poop into a jar and happily put on a drip.

The doctor attending me was mid to late 40's and very creepy. I decided I'd leave the clinic after my 4th bag of fluids because I felt better and was weirded out by the intense stares of my doctor. As I was paying the bill, the doctor came over, dropped to one knee and asked me to marry him at the desk. I stuttered in shock that I was already was married. He was holding a jar of my poo in his hand, stood and then chucked it at the wall. The jar broke open and my watery specimen was literally smeared across the wall as he trudged off. The woman serving me bobbed her head from side to side as if we were discussing the weather and said 'its not personal madam, you look like his last wife.'

Glass shame

'I was in Nashville airport in the smoking room. I heard my name being called for my flight so I rushed out but instead of rushing through the door, I walked smack into the glass. When I opened the door the entire departure lounge was roaring with laughter.'

The Dashing Date

'I had a date with a fellow Brit in Medellin. I went to the bathroom and when I came back, I asked him if he had paid the bill and he replied 'yes'. We were going down some stairs when he suddenly shouted at me to run. Yes, the restaurant staff were running after us because he hadn't paid.'

A fear of farting in hostels

'When I arrived to stay in my first ever hostel in London, I realised I had an intense fear
farting in my sleep. I literally gave myself such bad constipation I had to go to hospital. It turns out an enema is worse than hostel farting.'

What a boob

I fell on the Tube in London getting into a carriage. Unfortunately I managed to grab a woman's boob on the way to the floor. I was so mortified I walked everywhere else during the trip.'

Cementing a few laughs

'I was walking on the streets in Singapore when they were fixing the roads. I somehow stepped in fresh cement. I only noticed when my feet became so heavy I thought I had twisted my ankle. The cement got so hard, I had to take them off as I couldn't pick up my feet. Locals were very clearly entertained as I walked in my sponge bob squarepants socks.

If you've got a hilarious travel story you'd love to share, email me at   . All identifying details will be removed.

How I got hooked on budget travelling

'We're on holiday' is what my dad used to say to justify getting us in so much debt we lost our home and all our things when I was 11. We moved from the suburban bliss of Hemel Hempstead to a run down council estate in inner-city London, near my dad's new job as a refuge collector, a fancy word for dustbin man. I lost all my school friends while watching my dad go through a nervous breakdown.

My dad loved walking up a hotel lobby desk without a care in the world. So much so, that he booked overpriced holidays on credit cards. A lot of holidays. As it turned out we couldn't afford any of them. In the end, my dad had no choice but to declare bankruptcy. When my mum realised he'd racked up so much debt our family unit dissolved. A neat and perhaps as painless a summary of events that lead me to my life's passion: budget travel that doesn't compromise on fun, safety or comfort.

I started travelling full-time at the age of 18. I wrote the first Super Cheap Insider guide for friends visiting Norway - which I did for a month on less than $250. When sales reached 10,000 I decided to form the Super Cheap Insider Guides company. As I know from first-hand experience debt can be a noose around our necks, and saying 'oh come on, we're on vacation' isn't a get out of jail free card.

Before I embarked upon writing Super Cheap Insider guides many, many people told me that my dream was impossible, travelling on a budget could never be comfortable. I hope this guide has proved to you what I have known for a long-time: budget travel can feel luxurious when you know and use the insider hacks.

And apologies, if I depressed you with my tale of woe. My dad is now happily remarried and works as a chef in London at a fancy hotel - the kind he used to take us too!

A final word...

There's a simple system you can use to think about budget travel. In life we can choose two of the following: cheap, fast or
quality. So if you want it Cheap and fast you will get a
lower quality service. Fast-food is the perfect example. The system holds true for purchasing anything while travelling. I always
choose cheap and quality, except in times where I am really limited on time. Normally you can make small tweaks to make this
work for you. Ultimately you must make choices about what's
most important to you.

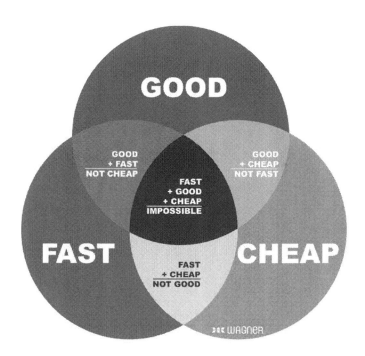

Our Writers

Phil Tang was born in London to immigrants, Phil graduated from The London School of Economics with a degree in Law. Now he travels full-time in search of travel bargains with his wife, dog and 1 year old daughter.

Ali Blythe has been writing about amazing places for 17 years. He loves travel and especially tiny budgets equalling big adventures nearly as much as his family. He recently trekked the Satopanth Glacier trekking through those ways from where no one else would trek. Ali is an adventurer by nature and bargainist by religion.

Michele Whitter writes about languages and travel. What separates her from other travel writers is her will to explain complex topics in a no-nonsense, straightforward way. She doesn't promise the world. But always delivers step-by-step methods you can immediately implement to travel on a budget.

Kim Mortimer, Kim's input on Super Cheap Insider Guides show you how to stretch your money further so you can travel cheaper, smarter, and with more wanderlust. She loves going over land on horses and helps us refine each guide to keep them effective.

Copyright

If you've found this book useful, please consider leaving a short review on Amazon it would mean a lot.

HOW DID WE DO?

1 DID WE SAVE YOU MONEY?

2 DID YOU LEARN INSIDER INSIGHTS?

3 DID YOU GET A LIST OF THE BEST CHEAP EATS?

4 DID WE HELP YOU PLAN TO SAVE AND ENJOY MORE?

WHAT CAN WE DO BETTER?

EMAIL ME: PHILGTANG@GMAIL.COM

Where NEXT?

ZURICH · VENICE · PRAGUE · MILAN · MARRAKESH · AUSTIN · CAPPADOCIA · EDINBURGH · ANTARCTICA

SUPERCHEAPINSIDERGUIDES.COM

Made in the USA
Coppell, TX
17 June 2021

57572730R00079